D0518958

A DOUBLE SORROW

A Double Sorrow

Troilus and Criseyde

LAVINIA GREENLAW

FABER & FABER

First published in 2014
by Faber & Faber Ltd
Bloomsbury House
74–77 Great Russell Street
London WC1B 3DA

Typeset by RefineCatch Ltd, Bungay, Suffolk
Printed in England by Martins the Printers

A CIP record for this book
is available from the British Library

ISBN 978-0-571-28454-2

FSC
www.fsc.org
MIX
Paper from
responsible sources
FSC® C101712

2 4 6 8 10 9 7 5 3 1

Go, litel bok, go, litel myn tragedye
V. 1786

Contents

Introduction

The story is simple. Boy meets girl, they fall in love, fate intervenes. They are victims of circumstance, timing, each other and themselves. Their story takes place within a city under siege in the midst of a long, intractable war. There are walls within walls, actual and otherwise.

The Trojan War was part of the Ancient Greeks' ancient history, events said to have taken place a thousand or more years before. Troy did, and didn't, exist. Even the Greeks had trouble finding it. It was part of a series of cities on a hill by the sea in Anatolia. The sea has long since retreated and Anatolia has dissolved into Turkey but the site remains.

The seeds of war, like those of tragedy, are usually a series of consequences. In this case, an impossible judgement and a dangerous promise. Paris, son of the Trojan king Priam, was forced to choose the loveliest among three goddesses. As reward he was offered the most beautiful woman in the world, and set off to claim her. She was Helen, wife of King Menelaus of Sparta. Her abduction (or, as would be asked of Criseyde, did she go willingly?) led Menelaus to rally an army to fetch her back. The Greeks arrived at Troy and surrounded the city.

The story of the siege of Troy is told in Homer's *Iliad*, which also contains the earliest extant mention of Troilus. A prince, and Paris's brother, he turns up before that in various stories in which his role is usually that of extreme youth and early death. Otherwise, he is remarked upon for his valiance. Medieval poets took hold of these old tales and established a practice of free borrowing and blithe reinvention, material now known as the Matter of Troy, an accumulation of versions and variations and component parts.

Troilus was given his own story, that of falling in love with a woman called Briseida, by the French poet Benoît de Sainte-Maure in his twelfth-century epic, *Roman de Troie*. This was adapted into a Latin prose version around 1287 by Guido delle Colonne, whose harsh view of Briseida set a lasting tone. Around 1340, the story was rendered into Italian poetry by Giovanni Boccaccio as *Il Filostrato* or 'the one rendered prostrate by love'. Boccaccio broke down the romance into steps and strategies – like a war or a dance – evolved Briseida into Criseida, and introduced Pandarus, the go-between.

Chaucer completed his version around 1383, the year he turned forty. He was at the height of his powers. *Troilus and Criseyde* is generally held to be his greatest work and in terms of English literature as important as *Beowulf* and Spenser's *Faerie Queen*. It stands alongside another great late-fourteenth-century poem, *Sir Gawain and the Green Knight*.

Although roughly two-thirds of Chaucer's text is original, he borrowed hugely from Boccaccio as well as from Guido and de Sainte-Maure, none of whom he acknowledges. Instead he credits a source called Lollius, whom he appears to have invented. Boccaccio, too, is coy about his own starting point.

Chaucer takes hold of this story as if he caught it in the air and freely incorporates what it brings to mind of his other reading. He read widely, and across languages, having translated the *Romance of the Rose* from French, and, from the Latin, Boethius's *Consolation of Philosophy*. He darkens Pandarus, casts a searching light on Troilus and listens to Criseyde. He goes to some lengths to remind us that he is not trying to provide any answers. Neither am I.

In activating rather than depicting courtly love, Chaucer unsettles everything, at times to the extent that things just don't add up. You find yourself wondering how Troilus can be hunting in the forest when under siege (Chaucer later mentions, as if in afterthought, that there had been a truce) and the denouement is pinned on the discovery of a brooch that you're not quite sure has been mentioned. They talk like medieval knights when they are ancient warriors, and refer to God but also to gods.

None of this matters. *Troilus and Criseyde* is the greatest account you will ever read of people arguing themselves and each other into and out of love. Like Boccaccio, Chaucer himself intervenes from the start. Whereas Boccaccio was asserting a personal connection, Chaucer is implicating us all: this is the lovers' story but it could be yours or mine. As for who does what and why, nothing is simple. Each imperative and response is shown to be made up of densely packed filaments: hope, fear, sympathy, pragmatism, self-protection, ambition, desire, exhaustion . . . I don't imagine that a fourteenth-century author was setting out in a twenty-first-century way to examine the lovers' psychology, but that in dramatising their relationship he drew out their inner processes.

Chaucer does this most forcefully through his imagery, much of which is borrowed from Boccaccio. What reads like an embroidered emblem in *Il Filostrato* is here brought to life, unfolding in front of us. It was the imagery, rather than the story, that made me want to write my own version – which is not a version, and certainly not a translation, but an extrapolation. I've jettisoned characters and scenes, and made some borrowings of my own. I've taken an image or phrase (which in the Chaucer may be a passing mention or something played out over hundreds of lines) and have used it to formulate each small but irrevocable step in the story. At times these are different aspects of the compacted emotions mentioned above. At others, they are decisions, gestures and (rarely) actions.

I've used a corrupt version of the form Chaucer chose for the poem, a seven-line stanza known as rime royal which has a rhyme pattern of A, B, A, B, B, C, C. It interests me that he untidied Boccaccio's neat eight-line verses (or octaves), and contrived a pattern that suggests circularity as much as development. Seven lines offer a sense of progression without conclusion and that fascinating fifth line doesn't quite fit. It's a spanner in the works; its echoing rhyme, a glance in the rear-view mirror.

The thread of the story runs above and below these poems through their titles and occasional subtitles, which I've placed at the foot of certain pages. These are an active and integral part of a work in which the margins are open and which was conceived overall as a form of detonation. I, too, have caught the story in the air and want to keep it there.

I was also encouraged by the resilience of this story and how over time, and through all its variations, its drama has deepened. The warrior prince, at first no more than a cipher, is filled out as a man trapped by convention in Boccaccio's hands and then, in Chaucer's, a man trapped in himself.

Troilus, '*Il filostrato*', does not fall in love. He falls down, he is felled. The framework of his life gives way, for all its structures, and until Pandarus appears to make things happen, he cannot act. He never quite grasps the idea that love is not a battle campaign, requiring only a strategy, and he never seems to wonder who Criseyde is beyond her beauty and fitness as the subject of a quest.

Who is she, this Briseida/Criseida/Criseyde who has surfaced through these retellings? '[A]n hevenyssh perfit creature,/That down were sent in scornynge of nature.' Someone too beautiful, unearthly, whose presence makes those around her feel ordinary. But who is she? A widow without children, of some nobility but not equal to royalty, whose father Calchas has betrayed Troy and abandoned her to go over to the enemy. But who is she? A woman of uncertain age, 'Tendre herted, slydynge of corage', trapped in a besieged city.

Her response to Troilus is never less than reasonable and often more realistic than his declarations and dreams. When she is handed over to the Greeks, at her father's urging, in an exchange of prisoners, he fails to speak up, telling himself he must above all protect her honour. They turn the matter over in a last night together, during which their absolute belief in each other is shown to be walled in (again, all kinds of walls) by doubt, fear, confusion, self-preservation. They hesitate and equivocate. It is all very human and very real.

When Criseyde arrives among the Greeks, her father subsides into the background. Once again alone she is preyed upon by the warrior sent to fetch her, Diomede. Unlike Troilus, who looks at her, Diomede reads her. At one extraordinary moment, he even asks her what she thinks (about the war), but this act of respect proves to be just another weapon. He is no less calculating than Troilus is self-regarding.

It is of course in the end not Troilus and Criseyde that make us weep but what we find of ourselves within them. For this story to have been passed so loosely across the centuries while losing nothing of its force is a reflection of the way in which stories outgrow and survive us by being about us at a far deeper level than any stories of our own.

LAVINIA GREENLAW

Note on the Text

Book and line numbers refer to Chaucer's *Troilus and Criseyde*.
IF indicates that the source is Boccaccio's *Il Filostrato*.

I would like to thank my editor Matthew Hollis for all he has done to make this peculiar work more itself rather than less so; and Jonathan Reekie, for room of my own.

– LG

A DOUBLE SORROW

BOOK ONE

A double sorrow

A sad story is sad to tell
But if it makes some part of sadness clear
To those who've suffered then it's real and therefore
True and we who've suffered can trace the shape
Of our own despair and so the shadow lifts
Leaving an outline that could be anyone's.
Take it or make it mine.

I. 1—21

5]

A prayer

For lovers
For those who do not remember
For those who do not recover
For those trapped in another's gravity
For those in love with love's certainties
For those who forget what is fixed must break
For love to be more than for love's sake.

I. 22–42

A thousand ships

As if the sea itself surrounds the city.
Why not? A brother's wife has been taken.
Seven years without breath or pity. Heart-stopped.
A brother's pride has been broken.
Trapped in the walls of this other story
An argument that has outgrown its truth
Why not argue themselves into love?

I. 57–63

7]

Calchas

Renowned for the scientific nature
Of his divinations, he sees that Troy will fall
And sees no future
And sees a truth he cannot tell
And sees that it is valuable.
So he takes to the Greeks what we all want to hear:
There is nothing to fear.

I. 64–84

Criseyde's father betrays Troy and flees

A loophole

What tempted the visionary?
Why would he go over to the enemy?
The people want him roast to the bone
Him and all his kin.
No one dares ask what he has seen.
Who among them is not losing hope?
Who is not looking for excuse, escape?

I. 85–91

Criseyde

Her beauty, so bright as to blank our gaze,
Empties the room.
In her presence we know ourselves most
Ordinary. She stands apart, is left alone.
A widow (why no child?) and now a traitor's daughter.
She knows what it means for her.
This is a small town.

I. 92–105

Slub

She throws herself before Prince Hector
Shimmering with fear. He takes her in
As if running cloth between his fingers:
Of some nobility, husband dead (why no child?)
On her knees, small like a small word.
The court whispers of the rich thread
And modest lustre of her dress – so well chosen.

I. 106–112

Criseyde hurries to the palace

Small words

Perhaps he is easily touched
But this woman is of such unusual beauty
And in war how often is there opportunity
To relish an act of chivalry, of delicatesse?

Your father has done us great injury.
He is cursed now. Let him go. But feel no less
At home. You will be treated with respect. I insist on it.

I. 110–123

Hector offers Criseyde his protection

Locked

She leads a winter life.
Staying put so as to hold her place
Like the city to which she belongs.
The nights are locked and the days are done.
Wherever she sets foot is ice.
She treats each person with excessive care
And they respect her.

I. 127–133

13]

Nothing moves

Things fall as they fall in war.
The wheel tips and the city pushes.
The wheel tips and the Greeks press.
Luck rolls back and forth.
Nothing moves
That does not then move on.
The days pass.

I. 134–140

Full well arrayed

The meadows beyond the walls are clothed
In new green, new pink, new sweetness.
Troy gathers for the feast of Pallas.
The high, the low and all between at their best:
Girls in their freshness, women in their brightness
Men in their fullness striding out and staring
As if walking the fields they could not walk that spring.

I. 155–168

A feast day in April

What men might in her guess

Among these candy colours stands Criseyde
A white veil above her widow's black.
The crowd acknowledge her natural place
As before all others – only she holds back
Hovering near the temple doors.
Under such dark clouds so bright a star
For being so defined uncertain all the more.

I. 169–182, 286

Troilus

Young soldiers – who've seen a thing or two
These last seven years – swirl down the street.
It's a feast day and here comes the sun
Lifting her skirt above her ankles. A little heat
And the fuse is lit. Except in him.
He judges some fair enough, some wanting
And does not burn in the taking or leaving.

I. 183–189

He's heard it all before

Although he keeps a close watch on his men
Some young lovely will have one bedazzled.
He predicts the same old story:
Days dreamt away and the long nights empty
While she sleeps sweetly.
It will end and it will happen again.
No one heeds such warnings.

I. 190–203

He raises his eyes to the heavens

As if for a moment he doubts the wisdom
Of having declared himself immune.
As if the god of love might be provoked into
Proving his bow unbroken.
Might select his sharpest arrow
Take aim at this complacent heart
And shoot.

I. 204–210

So we set out

As sure of where we're going as if climbing stairs.
Not noticing how one step leads to another
And step by step we're heading somewhere
Entirely other.
High hopes or none, we've no idea where we are
Until the stairs come to a stop
And the only way on is down not up.

I. 211–217

As if already

His men spill in feinting and flirting.
Troilus plays along while watching that none cross
A line. His gaze flits and swerves and falls upon
Criseyde just as she draws her veil about her face
And turns away. He feels the pull of himself
Propelled towards her, outside himself
If not beside her. As if already anchored there.

I. 266–273

The city gathers at the temple

A subject

So composed
Her every gesture confirms her grace.
Of such noblesse
A perfect woman, perfectly made.
(He only glimpsed her face.)
The prince must hide this joy, this fright.
He's never felt so full, so light.

I. 276–294

Deep in his heart her image is fixed

Her veil slips. He looks no further.
His men are forgotten.
His attention folds like a dying star
As he takes her – black and white – to his core.
The service begins.
He can neither see nor hear.
The people fall to prayer.

I. 295–301

Lime

His men gather him up.

He must play his part in the pranks and pleasures to come.

The day, the night, will be long.

He who takes flight without thought

Has to haul out of himself each word, each gesture

As love spreads through him like lime through feathers

And settles its weight.

I. 323–357

Troilus cannot move

What it is that pours from his heart

That he is lucky to find a woman who so deserves
His love. That the story of his love will be told
And that the story of his love will be no less glorious
If he fails.
That he can serve his love — whatever she feels —
And that if he can admit to having been shot through
Who will not admire his gaping wound?

I. 367–378

Seed

Night follows night.
His secret so full he cannot risk a sigh.
The air might creep with feeling.
What if someone – and there is always someone – close by
Were to taste it on their tongue and pass it on?
What fruit could grow from sweetness spread so thin?
Night follows night.

I. 384–385

Troilus cannot sleep

There is work to be done

Something to build strong enough to contain
The bird in his heart
That the wound has become.
He thinks of love as steps to a dance
And keeps breaking into song.
Rough-voiced
He must arm himself.

I. 381–389

Troilus attempts a strategy

If he ever fears he might not win her

He falls into some inward place of trees
Refusing any path that does not make of itself
The right answer. Hope will emerge
Like a gentle creature drawn from green shadows
To steady his gaze.
A fawn, soft in the wild,
Followed only by more of its kind.

I. 463–466

The sharp showers fall

He will not flinch or swerve.
In at the first, there to the last,
He sees it all from on high
Like a god. He sees this war is small.
Indifferent, invincible, sleepless, tireless
He thinks of the stories they'll tell.
How could she then say no?

I. 470–484

Troilus in battle

Vapours

Whispering long ribbons of fear.
Reveries and sighs. At the fall of her name
He gives way like snow flung upon a fire.
People wish this?
He does not know that what he feels is feeling.
Should he declare himself? What is correct?
If so, not yet.

I. 435–462, 523–525

Troilus hesitates

Pandarus

A man who wanders the corridors
Who presses his ear to the wall
Who rushes in as if to the rescue.
Has the prince – flat out, sobbing – been hurt
Or has some devilry borne fruit?
He pulls up a chair.
He can taste the juice.

I. 547–560

At his friend's insistence

I fear that to put this into words
Will break me down
But I must show you trust
So here it is. I love someone
And do not want this weakness
To be known. A thousand ships
Have sailed into my heart. Say nothing.

I. 596–616

Troilus speaks

Whet

Why have you kept this to yourself for so long?
My trials in love are renowned.
To be blunt
I've learnt what should – and should not – be done.
I may be well worn but I know how to sharpen.
Think of me as an instrument
On which to tune your song.

I. 617–632

Pandarus gives himself a role

Hover

This brother, this passer-by
Sees the highs and lows to come
And as he has no adventure of his own
Anticipates the sport:
How they will hover at the ready
Till she's drawn forth.
How they will soar and swoop.

I. 670–671

34]

Yet he nothing answers

He struggles to raise his head
Then subsides back into lethargy
Till his friend roars

                    Wake up!
Has fear folded up your breath?
So young, so green, so vigorous!
Serve this love. Devote yourself.
Are you not ready?

I. 722–730, 800–819

Troilus is challenged

Dropped

He's on the edge of a precipice.
At its foot, dark water.
Who knows what lies beneath or if
He will survive the fall.
This is his trial.
He must name his grail.
He names her.

To love well and in a worthy place

Flawless, as you already know,
And while not quite your equal
Beyond peer in her gentility.
Made for romance and while not susceptible
She will be feeling a certain vulnerability.
If there's love in her then love we'll find.
We just need to pinpoint what kind.

I. 876–889, 974–987

Pandarus explains that Criseyde is his niece

To have someone speak of it as if it could be done

He is told to concentrate
To be patient, to rehearse
To suffer the tide and to have faith
That the right conditions will arise.
All weather is changeable.
There will be a path
And it will be passable.

I. 954–961

Troilus listens

As a gentleman

If I have any fear
It is that I may be the cause
Of damage to her.
I will only go so far as is proper.
I put myself in your hands.
Commend me to she who me commands
But do not use force.

I. 1030—1057

Troilus draws a line

A construct

First measure out the work.
Do not rush into laying foundations.
Read the lie of the land
And draw whatever line you take
As if from the heart.
The right words will lend grace
To the right time and the right place.

I. 1065–1071

Pandarus gives himself some advice

High

He gallops out on his bay
And in battle is ever more brave
As if under a form of protection.
Otherwise he's changed.
Remember his mockery? His disdain?
His thoughtfulness is remarked upon.
He may never be himself again.

I. 1072–1085

Troilus wakes

BOOK TWO

Out of these black waves for to sail

This plot (which has not been easy to steer)
Is finding its course.
The air has started to clear
For better or worse.
The prince and his friend are learning to rhyme
What might be said with where and when.
So it begins. Day one.

II. 1–10

A form of speech

Stories change shape in the telling
As words alter through long use.
This is nothing new
But it's close to home
Which might colour my view (were I to have one).
It's not exactly light, not entirely dark.
I'm saying what happens not naming parts.

II. 15–24

The second of the four sweet months

The meadows quicken.
Life drifts across the walls.
What's inside opens.
Consider the phase of the moon
The sun full-beam in the sign of the bull
The sharpness of the swallow's song.
The time has come.

II. 50—75

47]

Imperative

Listening in sleep to the swallow's song
He hears small wheels in a vast machine
Doing their best to keep up.
Less of a beat, more of a ripple.
Something's got caught. It spins and slaps.
He opens the back
And out comes spool after spool.

II. 64–68

Pandarus remembers his promise

Forgetful of all measurement

He yells for his servants to dress him now
And bulging with intent bounds forth
Without thought of what he might say
Or she.
He marches through his niece's gates
As if he were about to rescue the people
From seven years' battle.

II. 71–80

Within a paved parlour

She is at home among women
One of whom is reading aloud
A well-known tragedy:
A king's death, the terrible act of a son
And a world where too much happens
And not enough to some. They laugh at it
But each is on the edge of her seat.

II. 81–105

Sits Criseyde among her companions

A red-letter day

He yanks her to her feet
Grinning as if about to announce the greatest
Good news.

Why indoors? Have you not seen the sun?
We must pay observance. Dance! Dance!

Uncle, please don't rave.
You're scaring me.

II. 103, 111–116

Barb

Take off the scarf drawn tight beneath your chin.
It hangs like a beard. Unbutton!

You know why I cover myself.
I am a widow, no longer womanly.
I should live in a cave and devote my days
To religious tracts. I cannot caper and twirl.

Still he caws: Oh lucky girl, lucky girl!

II. 110, 117–118

52]

A corner

He sits her down as if about to announce whatever
It is but says that if he were able to tell her
There is something he could tell her
That would make her dance
Then he takes a sharp turn
Towards himself, the weather, the old romance
She's reading and its other dozen versions . . .

II. 108, 121–133

Pandarus leads Criseyde out of earshot

Till she can bear no more and turns back

What is this great good luck?
This secret you're trying so hard to keep.
Are the gates open? Are we without enemy?
Please don't play games.
I find it hard to keep up.
Your poetry strains.
Just tell me.

II. 122–154

The king has more than one son

He winds one brother round the other
Speaks of Hector's latest skirmish
And out of it the other's splendour:
Troilus in superlatives.
This is not news, she's already heard
From those to whom she most pays heed
All about this man, this shield.

II. 155–189

Glaze

Now the prince's name is in the air
His friend keeps it spinning
Till noble deeds and bright lines blur
And neither crack nor fault can be discerned
In his image.
Judging the picture complete
He rises and says that he must leave.

II. 190–209

A serious matter

He thinks he has her but she wants only
Advice on the management of her money.
He tries to say the right things.
When her accounting comes to an end
He leaps up. They have to dance
Because Fortune has made her the offer
Of a future. And what a future!

II. 210–224

Criseyde says they must talk further

The strength in any story lies in its end

His theme demands elaboration
So on he rambles till his eyes fix upon her face
And he sees it clearly:
Her simplicity.
He takes the decorations down.

You're being given a chance, he says.
Take it.

II. 246–294

He who strives to do right in all things

The noble Troilus does so love you
That his life is hell. In truth
I do not believe he will survive
His longing. There it is.
Do as you wish. Have him live or die.

She knows that life is about to change
And that in change lies danger.

II. 309–322

A knife

Say no and he will die
And I who failed to save his life
Will slit my throat with this very knife.
The prince and I offer only protection.
Imagine us gone. Feel how sharp the blade.
Such a man thrown away
As if he were *ordinary*.

II. 323–340

Pandarus presses

A stone

He warns her that her charms won't stretch
To making amends for the prince's loss.
She may be beauty's root and crop
But like the most precious crystal
If she lacks the power to heal
Where's the use?
She neither moves nor speaks.

Transparency

If he came to her door it would not be often.
He knows how to govern himself.
Yes people might talk so why not be open?
This would be the visit of a friend.
No promises.
Just a little kindness.
The city is full of such friends.

II. 365–380

Pandarus releases

She turns the colour of the morning air

This is it? My great good luck?
Were I misguided enough to declare a passion
For a man of royal blood, for any man
Given who I am, you would be merciless
And I would be a laughing stock.
What is this painted process?
You call this a happy ending. In what version?

II. 410–427, IF *II. 47*

Criseyde reddens

Jeopardy

I must play my cards well
Or this will prove a dangerous game.
It might make things worse if I refuse to listen.
I've heard of the extremes men go to for love.
What if the prince killed himself?
What if he came here and slit his throat in front of me?
What would people say?

II. 456–462

Criseyde thinks

Yes

I will not offer him my hand.
I will not lead him here.
I cannot love him if I do not love him.
Else I will try to light his day
As I can do so honourably.
I say now I will offer nothing more
Even if it destroys him, you, me.

II. 477–489

Criseyde decides

A puzzle

She lays out what's been said
Turning each word over.
All she can remember.
She arranges shapes
And sees how pieces might fit together
And is astonished to find her fear gone
And this thing become what will happen.

II. 600–606

Criseyde retires to her chamber

Undone is the chain

The street on which she lives is closed
Yet now come shouts to give access
To what's left of a company of soldiers
In need of a shortcut back to the palace.
She hears the clop and clank and groans
The horses pulling like tired machines
Nothing from the men inside their armour.

II. 611–623

Prowess

The gloss of his bay running red
The prince still full richly dressed
Bows his head. His mangled helmet
Dangles by a thread like a piece of tin.
His shield tough with sinew, hide and horn
Is scored and hacked and arrow-pierced.
The people chant his name regardless.

II. 624–647

Troilus in defeat

She lets him sink softly into her heart

Drawn to her window by his name
She thinks herself the only one to notice
His cheeks burn. He looks to the ground.
He will not play to the crowd.
She thinks how urgently he needs to lie down
Somewhere quiet and warm among silk and feathers
And she blushes.

II. 645–650

Gently

This sight sets off in her
A gathering of all she knows.
His charms roll smoothly back and forth
But what comes to rest
Is herself as the cause of his distress.
She takes this in – so moved
That it starts to translate itself into love.

II. 651–665

A basis

You can hear the envious
Condemning this sudden change of heart
At the sight of him battle-scarred
But every love must find its start.
It's only that she now feels more inclined
Towards him. Think of her as a fortress
Being slowly undermined.

II. 666–679

Angles

She takes up the matter
As if it were to be folded like paper.
I am my own woman. No longer wife
And at ease to be so. This is the right life
I am in. At home amongst women.
Yet he is the king's son
And a place to rest my heart upon.

II. 694–764

Glare

Haven't I seen what love does?
Like the sun it cannot help its brightness
And so blinds us.
A woman is exposed
While a man can stand in shadow.
His love came out of nowhere.
It will go there.

II. 778–798, 862–863

Criseyde anticipates

Courage

Come darkness things slip out of shape.
She dreams an eagle with bone-white feathers
Opens her chest with his long fingers
Removes her heart and puts in place his own.
She has no fear and feels no pain.
Heart for heart to keep.
Now let her sleep.

II. 905–932

74]

Should he weep or sing?

Home from that day's skirmish he wants only news
And takes nothing of all that's brought to him.
He is told to eat, to rest. The net has been cast
And a promise has been drawn:
To be his loving friend.

What does that mean? I'm held by this as by a noose
And I am dangling.

II. 933–962, 985–987

Troilus asks

A frame

She stands at the window but turns away.
Every now and then she
Looks over her shoulder down towards where he
Waits. She knows he waits.
Her glance is neither proud nor punitive.
The greater hope, the greater love.
He will not move.

IF *II. 82, 85*

Criseyde shows herself

He is at first content with her courtesy

Seven years in a locked city
And each time she equals his gaze
He's in a new place.
A thousand cities construct themselves
Within him. Avenues unfurl.
He turns each corner but meets only
Wall on wall on wall.

II. 977–978, IF *II. 82, 85*

He can live near her no longer

When she leaves my sight I cannot rest
Till I have her in front of me again. Alight
I am forced back to the flame.
I must act.

Now is not the time.
Try to do what I say
Or charge someone else with your destiny.

II. 981–994, IF *II. 89*

Troilus insists, Pandarus obstructs

The art of poetry

If you must do something now write a letter.

I do not have the art and am sure to offend her.

Use fine words but don't reiterate.
Neither too neat nor too ornate.
Don't spin arguments or put on airs.
Use the right terms. This is love not war.
Let an inkblot fall – like a tear.

II. 1005–1043

Lines

Dear lady, the thought of you prowls through me
And hunts out any other that might bring to mind
Another. Or anything. You are so very
— he recalls the terms —
Pleasing, delightful, blissful, kind.
The cure for my pain.
I who am — he knows it's a lie — unworthy.

II. 1065–1085, IF *II. 99*

Troilus finds the words

Like an oriental pearl

She inspires awe as much as desire.
Her charms so extreme
They make of her a stranger.
Made of what stuff?
Water or fire or earth?
What brought her here?
Few dream of holding her.

IF *II. 108*

81]

A cage

He turns up at dawn waking everyone.

She begs him: Do not bring me this.

So he thrusts it into her breast.
She says aloud that she will not read these words
Then, folding it away, makes some excuse.
Her days are filled with talk of such tameness
That the prince's words are lions.

II. 1128–1178

Pandarus delivers Troilus's letter, Criseyde reads it

A door half open

She is told that she must offer words of her own.
Her uncle can provide them.
But she takes herself away from all scrutiny
And writes what she does not know she will say.
She thanks him for all he has well meant towards her.
She will not make promises or give up her liberty.
She offers herself as sister.

II. 1195–1225

Jasper

He settles himself among gold cushions
And starts to say that though a woman hard won
Is not easily forgotten
Now is the time.
He leans in.
Her fingers trace the flow of light and dark
Trapped in the stone beneath them.

II. 1227–1239

Though Criseyde has replied, Pandarus will not be gone

A veil

Her letter is in his hands.
His spirits rise and fall. And rise.
He decides that on balance she says yes
But that she does not yet know what to do
With what she feels.
To him her words are a veil.
He tries to read through them.

II. 1318–1328

Troilus interprets

Dice

He decides he has a fair chance
And writes each day.
She might be sweet, might be fierce
If she deigns to reply.
After such answer as he has
He writes again.
She says that she is now more his than her own.

II. 1331–1341, IF *II. 131, 136*

An axe

She remains upright.
Her dignity
is rigid and deep-rooted.
The prince is told to think of an oak
And how any fool might hack away.
What matters is the felling stroke
Then it's all over in one great sway.

Pandarus describes an approach

Prescriptions

The prince is instructed to fall ill
And then to take to bed.
He is anyway so evidently tormented, so pale.
Each of the guests knows what he needs:
A potion, an amulet, an incantation, certain herbs . . .
She says nothing. It pleases her
To know that she alone has the cure.

II. 1572–1582

A dinner is contrived at which they meet

A small room is easily warmed

He files his tongue smooth
And setting her somehow aside
From the company persuades her
To visit the prince in his borrowed chamber.
She should enter the curtains alone
So as not to strain the air.
He leads her deeper.

II. 1646–1681

Pandarus takes Criseyde to see Troilus

And inward thus

He takes up the hem of her sleeve
And says nothing as he guides her
Along dark corridors.
Enough pursuit, enough delay
He hopes this romance can now begin
And that she will waste no more time
On what others might think or see or say.

II. 1732–1750

BOOK THREE

Love on earth

It comes in a thousand forms.
A bull rises out of the sea.
A swan plunges. A gold rain falls.
Or a noble heart perceives in itself
Divine agency.
What else is life?
Seize it.

III. 1–21

A weakness

He has rehearsed his lines all evening
Yet when she lays a hand upon his arm
The words bolt
And his cheeks boil red.
He shakes.
He cannot speak.
And she adores this in him.

III. 50–88

What does he want?

I do not know what you want me to say
Or be. You ask for mercy
As if I'm inflicting some kind of punishment
When I offer pity
And have promised to be your loving friend.
I'm grateful for your protection
But it's never been clear what you intend.

III. 76–77, 120–126

Criseyde tries to ask

Know my patience

Only that now and then
You turn those lovely eyes my way
And look upon me kindly
And that you trust in my modesty
My truth and diligence
And allow me to be your first resort in all things.
Seek my help at any hour for any reason.

III. 127–144

Troilus tries to answer

So far as is right

In good grace she accepts his service
Within the bounds of honour
And of such love as this is.
She will hold back nothing
That might him yet recover. She offers her lips
And all the bells of the city chime
In that little room.

III. 155–189

Bawd

I shall put you in her arms but tell no one.
There are a thousand stories of a woman's reputation lost
Through a man's boasts.
Were it known
What I have contrived . . . I would be
Condemned and she would lose her name.
She would be nothing. You would have won nothing.

III. 240–280, IF *III. 10*

Pandarus leads Criseyde back and returns alone

Green

Who can tell even half the delight he feels.
So parched had he become, so densely drawn
All hiding places.
Now each holt and hedge in him
Runs green again
Restored to the impulse
That had woken him in spring.

III. 344–356

99]

He sees his lady sometime

They are careful
And barely speak when they meet.
He makes much of what little they have
And fights fiercely.
At night he turns on his pillow
Devising countless ways
To serve the one he dreams of seizing.

III. 451–459

Presence

She has no cause to request or refuse
Since he anticipates each command.
He places himself like steel between
Her and all she has found
So troubling.
She's more relieved than afraid.
No one is asking her now to choose.

III. 464–483

Out of doubt

He evaluates each glance and gesture
Takes note, balances the books
And sees that the lovers need to consolidate
These rushed moments
And that this will require a place
Of which they can be certain.
A place to which only he can lead them.

III. 512–532

Pandarus concludes

Ordinance

He waits downwind
And hones his alibi.
If anyone asks why he spent the night away
He will allude to the temple
And how he must sit alone in vigil
Waiting for Apollo to speak in the trembling of the laurel
Of when to expect surrender.

III. 533–546

Troilus is kept informed

When lightless is the world

A scrape of moon in a heaped sky.
Despite the coming storm
She crosses town with full retinue, properly,
To dine with her uncle. He has insisted:

Come tonight or never again.

                           He lays on a feast.
Nothing that could have been hoped for is missing.
He sings, she plays, he tells the old stories.

III. 549–616

Pandarus commands Criseyde to dine with him

Black rain

This conjunction of the bent moon
With Saturn and Jupiter in the house of Cancer
Occurs once every six hundred years.
Crab weather: the world lagooned
And things forced sideways.
The streets unpassable. Wherever
You are tonight, stay put.

III. 624–644

As far as possible from the storm

She who lives in fear of getting caught out
Cannot get home. Her uncle offers her
The quietest place: an inner room beyond his.
Her ladies will occupy the connecting chamber.
Having taken care of proprieties
They drain the last glass
And she is put to bed.

III. 659–693

The lover in his hiding place

Her host is sure-footed. This is just
Another version of a dance he knows well.
He steps lightly – first to slide back the bolt
Behind which the prince has been concealed
In the stew. Hours in that rank closet
Yet this mouse has to be cajoled
(Too pitter-patter) into coming forth.

III. 694–737

The roar

He leads the quailing prince to a little trap door
Then makes him wait while he slides himself into
Her chamber. She wakes, sees her uncle and moves
To fetch a chaperone.

His whisper stops her.
They would only reach the wrong conclusion.
Her life is a room within rooms.
Beyond – the wild wind.

III. 743–764

Pandarus delivers Troilus to Criseyde

How this candle in the straw has fallen

This is a most urgent and delicate matter.
Think of it as being rescued from a fire.
Your lover has broken into this house ablaze
With the rumour that you have extended a promise
To another. You must convince him otherwise.
Not in the morning. Now.
His mind is alight. Now.

III. 796–917

Pandarus persuades Criseyde to see Troilus

Tryst

Her heart turns cold in wonder
That her love could hold her false so lightly
That someone would tell such a lie
That she dared to feel joy.
She considers all things as they stand
And what it means to be good.
Her heart turns cold in wonder.

III. 799–889

Cushions

And then he is suddenly there
And her words not quick
But a kiss.
And all that is left to their broker
Is smoothing the silk and plumping the feathers.

Now you can begin. I'll be over there
Reading something or other.

III. 958–980

Grain

She gathers up the harm
His suspicions might have done
And seeks within this bushel the one pure grain
Of love.
It is enough.
Why can feelings not bear their own name?
He does not say this jealousy was an invention.

III. 1023–1050

The feeling of his sorrow

That she is made so distraught
By his deceit
Turns him upon himself
And he finds that there is nothing of himself
He can bear to keep.
All life in him has flown.
Derelict – he falls down.

III. 1065–1092

Troilus collapses

Wax

The prince lies at her feet.
She is instructed to help him onto the bed, to warm
His palms, his wrists, his temples, to rub, to dab
To stroke, to kiss, to reach an arm around him.
He finds a form.
Their friend sees that he can do no more
And carries off the candle.

III. 1114–1141

Pandarus takes charge

Aspen

He holds her so completely that she shakes.
This is what she's read about in books
But never known. The lightness
That comes from being free of doubt.
Willing the breeze.
About to be let go by the tree
Not to fall but float.

Shift

She moves away only to undress
Discarding her garments piece by piece
Till she stands in her shift
And – like a bride – hesitates
Then laughs:

Shall I free myself of this?

And she does.

IF *III. 31–32*

Honeysuckle

As about a tree with many a twist
They wind themselves into
A thousand tendrils.
The depth of each flower.
The fullness of detail.
The kiss upon kiss upon kiss
Being met, being equal.

III. 1230–1232

A nightingale

She cannot help but cry out
Only to stop as she starts
For fear of who's passing
Or what might be hidden within.
Then she breathes
And finding her voice
Shows him everything.

III. 1233–1239

In this heaven he starts to delight

A place of softest snow
A place of rise and fall
A place of open paths
A place of long curves
A place of pale cloud
A place of fine feathers
A place without walls.

III. 1247–1302

The slipping night

They will not sleep
But think themselves dreaming nonetheless
So perfected is this.
Minute by minute so complete
Each brings the question of the next:
Is this your true self?
What of this can I possibly keep?

III. 1338–1348, IF *III. 34*

Live certain of my love

At dawn they turn over the matter of parting
And play at an exchange of rings.
If he could be certain she will hold him
In mind. If she could believe herself fixed
In his. She takes a gold and azure brooch
Set with a ruby heart and pins it to his shirt
In outline.

III. 1366–1372, 1485–1499, IF *III. 49*

The idea of it

Returning home he slinks under the covers
Hoping for sleep but what comes is the night
Just gone. He sees it all so brightly
And she better lit than ever before.
Returning home she cannot stop speaking of him
To herself and weighs each second
That has to pass before they meet again.

III. 1534–1554, IF *III. 54–55*

Take up the thread

At last you're at ease
But do not look so triumphant.
You will need just as many strategies
To hold on to what you've won. Such joy
Is delicately bound. This is self-evident.
Think how hard it is to contain.
Tighten the knot.

III. 1615–1638

Pandarus points out to Troilus that this is not an end

BOOK FOUR

Luck

They are caught in Fortune's brightest gaze
And brightly lit must watch her turn away.
Her face drawn down and darkening
Into shadows and hollows
Like an old story
About the cost of beauty.
Betrayal. Blame. Who'd be a woman?

IV. 1–21, IF *III. 94*

The long day closes

At summer's breaking point
Hector gathers his best men and goes full out.
They burst onto the broad plains resplendent
With spears, maces, swords and axes.
About to win, they are misled.
The Greeks move in to kill or capture.
Those who survive must have fled.

IV. 30–49

An investment

The old king intervenes
To propose an exchange of prisoners.
The calculations are made: of mutual worth
And how any surplus value might be met.
In the Greek camp Calchas draws near
To those doing the sums. Hoping for a cut
He pitches his idea.

IV. 57–68

Priam takes command from Hector

A changed face

I came here with nothing more than my vision
Relinquishing my entire estate.
You know you'll win.
Do you also know I left a daughter sleeping?
What hardness in my heart refused to wake
Her – now defenceless and alone!
I should have dragged her here in her nightgown . . .

IV. 71–112

Calchas has tears in his eyes

Any day now

I have seen it in the oracle of Apollo, in the stars
In the auguries of birds, in the casting of lots.
When the city falls you will more than recoup your costs.
Why not give me one prisoner
With whom I can free my daughter?

In his cracked voice they hear a cracked heart.
They give him Antenor.

IV. 106–133

Safeguards

The king, his sons and all his lords
Dispute the Greek terms.
And it is said:
For Antenor they want the lady Criseyde.
Like the soldiers sent to guarantee passage
For the enemy ambassadors
Troilus demurs.

IV. 141–158

He turns over in himself

He must speak but he has promised
To tell no one of their affair.
How might he protect her honour?
How might he protect himself from the loss of her?
He does not have her permission to decide this.
Like a boat drifting towards a fork in a river
He does not know he wavers.

IV. 148–168, IF *IV. 14–16*

Chaff

The words that should come
Come from the mouth of his brother:

We do not sell our women.
She's no prisoner for barter.

Hector! Have you fallen
For the traitor's daughter?
We choose Antenor.

IV. 176–196

A dead image

His mind can do nothing with this
So carries it off. Mindless
He makes his way home, bolts the door
And puts out every lamp in his chamber
As if plucking the last bright leaves
From the blackest tree in winter.
He is branch and bark – the barest dark.

IV. 219–230, IF *IV. 21*

Troilus alone

A living creature

What he feels is of such size
And wiring
It must kick its way out
To survive him.
Excessively strong
And otherwise nothing
It throws him wall to wall.

IV. 239–259

Envy

The gods have looked upon this love
And decided the cost.
Could they not kill his father?
Or snatch one of his brothers?
Was this just to prove
How useless it is to be human?
How lost?

IV. 274–287

He prays that he might leave his body

My spirit unnest.

Fly to her and follow her.

Your right place is no longer here.

What is there to look on but her departure?

Not even the time to grow used to it.

I have cried myself out.

My eyes are noughts.

IV. 302–312

138]

To her father

I wish your corrupt blood had stopped your heart
As you hurried off. Mislived old man
I wish the Greeks had cut your gristly throat
When you proposed this trade.
Your life weighs too much
On mine. Come home
And I will separate us.

IV. 330–336

He sleeps and wakes

His friend is at a loss.
He stands in the dark
And folds his arms.

Why not be satisfied with the fact
That you've had what you wanted?
This town is full of women.
I could rustle up a dozen such . . .

IV. 344–406

Pandarus moves on

An abbreviation

New love is required to chase out the old.
A new approach for this new world.
Weeping won't keep her from leaving.
You need to put things in proportion.

At last the prince says something:
Your medicine, my friend,
Is cure for a fiend.

IV. 415–437

Now this, now that

As if I have been stung
And the cure is something fresh and green.
As if logic were an ingredient, there to add,
And love all air.

If that's how you feel then take her.
You're the son of the king.
Free to take what you dare.

IV. 461–530

All this have I thought

What have we become these last seven years
Because a woman was forced? I could approach my father
But that would make known all that's gone on.
He would say she is not of our blood
And that she must go for the city's good.
I must protect her honour
Even as I cannot protect her.

IV. 547–571

Troilus looks to the past and future

Divine not reason so deep

Wash your face and go about your business.
Return to court before the king starts to wonder
Where you are. In times of crisis
Things become a matter of rhetoric.
It's hardly force to withhold the one you love
And who loves you. And what of her?
Does she even know this deal's been struck?

IV. 589–656

Pandarus urges Troilus to act

Fact

The story of the deal spreads
Like a thousand birds released from a net.
A burst of flight then a breaking up into
Detail and innuendo.
Every bird finds a perch
Whether or not it deserves a place
In what's reported.

IV. 659–662

She has heard

Her women weep and say the right things
About being restored to her father
And how while they will miss her this will bring
Peace. She's not really there.
In her mind she's searching for him.
Trying to pin him down.
She can't find him.

IV. 687–700

What is Criseyde worth when from Troilus?

Weeping is not enough
And beating her breast is not enough
So she tears at the brightness of her hair
As if plucking beams from the sun.
She wants to put out her light
And for her spirit to stay here with him
As she departs – in outline.

IV. 736–780

Criseyde alone

Pass

Why does he not claim her
Through love or force?
How can her plaint be sung
When so out of tune?
What voice could contain the full dimensions
Of the noise she is making?
Who has the words?

IV. 799–805

From whom nothing is ever kept

Her uncle shoves his way into her room.
She cannot face him
And pulls her loosened hair across her eyes
As if trying to find a door to close.
He can't stand her pain – or the prince's –
And wants to get out fast. He tells her
To rise, to wash her face. It's all he has.

IV. 815–824

Hurt

How could any one person contain
Such agony?
So much torment there can be none left
Beyond this body.
All the world's woe, complaint, distress
Anguish, rage, dread and bitterness . . .
I have been made to take it all in.

IV. 841–847

Criseyde protests

About her eyes purple rings

She asks what word he might bring.
That the court has agreed the exchange.
That her lover is beside himself
And needs a night with her
So they might find an answer.
Her gaze comes from a place so dark
He tries not to return her look.

IV. 869–889

Criseyde faces Pandarus

A blade

Shape yourself.
To see you in such disarray
Would pierce his heart.
Smooth your face.
Flatten your sharps.
Take his line.
Press to him.

IV. 925–931

Pandarus continues to instruct Criseyde

He finds consolation in philosophy

What makes what happen?
Take a man in a chair. He knows he sits.
We who see him sit can say it's true
And was so meant but what if
It had been foretold and did not happen?
What if his life was the chair and it remained unmade
In the realm of the tree?

IV. 960–1078

Troilus sits

The consolation of his friend

She is not all you were made for.
Remember the years you did not know her
And were content. I have just seen her
And looking at you now must say
You do not feel half her pain.
Go when it is night
And make of this an end.

IV. 1093–1115, IF *IV. 111*

Pandarus reminds Troilus

They cannot speak for weeping

All she has been made to contain
Has forced such utterance
That what pours forth now is silence.
He holds a broken thing
And after a while arranges her
As if a mortician in search of the person.
Then he too lies down.

IV. 1135–1183

Troilus and Criseyde meet that night

They sleep, she wakes

I can withstand my father's wishes but not the king's.
I have to go but believe me that I can contrive
A way home. This will all die down
And every day there's more talk of peace.
It's half a day's ride.
Meanwhile I'll send news somehow.
I can be back in – what – ten days?

IV. 1275–1330

Ambiguities

We're not yet on firm ground
Nor are we in deep water
And as for my father
I'll persuade him the gods ordain my return
By finding a way to turn it into gold.
For now we're neither here nor there
So breathe.

IV. 1394–1406

From leaf to leaf

He brings himself to believe her
Because he loves her
And both feel lighter.
They turn to small things
Like a pair of birds
Who flit from spot to spot of sun
And chirp of each green landing.

IV. 1432–1435, IF *IV. 138*

Fantasy

He cannot escape her leaving and fears
Her father's sleight of hand
And fine talk from handsome men.
She will look back from among them
And see him as uncouth.
The city rough. She will not come home
And the siege will never be broken.

IV. 1470–1491

He runs away with himself

Why risk separation?
What fool gives up their very being?
Let's steal ourselves away.
We may lose reputation and betray
The king but I have kin elsewhere.
If we turned up in our bare shirts
We'd still be honoured guests. We can afford this.

IV. 1503–1526

Shall she be cursed

We would find ourselves too free.
No. You must let me go. But believe this:
The river that runs like an arrow
Through our city and down to the sea
Shall turn back upon its source
Should I prove false. And by god and man
and good and bad and beast shall I be cursed.

IV. 1527–1554

Ten days

People would say it was not an act of love
But one of fear and desire. We are at war.
You would lose your honour and I my name.
Stay here where I will be again
By the time the moon has carried itself
Out of the ram and into the lion.
You are a prince: strong enough to endure.

IV. 1555–1596

Unquestionable

Long after dawn they lie tight pressed.
At last he makes himself dress
All the while looking upon his lover
As if upon his death.
When he understands what is going to happen
His spirit tears itself out of his chest.
He leaves the room.

IV. 1688–1701

BOOK FIVE

Circles

The sun moves through its signs.
The day of her departure comes. At dawn
Diomede stands full ready to receive her.
Why does Troilus not defy his father
Abandon his brothers, kill this man and grab her?
He answers himself that she might get hurt in the fray.
He joins the crowd at the gate.

V. 8–56

The Greeks arrive to collect Criseyde

Who would not trust her sadness?

When Criseyde is ready to be gone
She turns to Diomede as he takes her reins
And says with great coldness:

I have shown myself long enough.
Let us not dwell.

She bids her servants farewell
Otherwise no one.

V. 57–63, IF *V. 8–9*

A courtesy

Troilus is alongside.
One among many.
He raises a gloved fist
On which sits a hooded hawk.
They ride out beyond the valley at a slow walk.
He would remain with her every step of the way
But turn he must.

V. 64–70

He manages himself

From among the Greeks comes Antenor.
The Trojans cheer. The prince tries
But he is fixed on she who is leaving.
He takes her right hand in his right hand
With great formality and whispers
That she must hold to the tenth day or he will die.
To the man taking her reins he says nothing.

V. 71–87

Diomede

He observes the prince's silence
The lady's grief, their barely touching hands
And sees that there is something in this
For him. He will drive out the other man.
All he has to do is understand.
Where the prince might sing to himself
He reads her.

V. 92–105

So soon away

They fall into conversation.
He makes of her distress a question:
Is there anything he can do that might
Put her at ease? He interrogates
The immediacy of his devotion
So that she doesn't. He will be her friend.
She needs one.

V. 100–140

Diomede leads

Enveloping

He waits till her father's tent is in sight
Then says he can guess what weighs on her
And that even those on opposite sides
Worship at the same altar
When it comes to love. He repeats his offer
Then seals the conversation
By pointing out her new home.

V. 120–151

They arrive at the Greek camp

A bluff

Then he turns and blurts about having never
Met a woman who so pierced his heart
Keeping his words abrupt
As if this were sudden exposure.
He presents his feelings as a shock:
The discovery in himself of an outcrop
Across which he now stumbles.

V. 155–175

Disappearance

She has been sinking all the while
And hears what he says from underwater.
She catches some words – *friendship, brother* –
And being who she is
Thanks him as she slips from her horse
And steps as a child
Back into the house of her father.

V. 176–194

Inside the walls of himself

No one dares speak to the prince
On his return, his face set so hard
Such anger in his manner.
Alone at last he gives vent to the loss
Of his happiness. He blames his fate, his birth
All possible gods. He sees no worth
In anything they've created beyond her.

V. 197–210

Troilus returns to the palace

Where am I where she is?

Where are her arms that last night were here?
Where is her body where?
Is this pillow all that's left for me to embrace?
How can I persevere?
Who right now stands in her presence?
To whom right now does she listen?
Who will speak for me right now in my absence?

V. 218–236

A pale horizon

There's just the faintest line of day
When he sends for his so-called brother
Who swears he would have come before
Had he not been detained on palace business.
He knows what to expect:
The prince sleepless, his woe endless.
The stars are still in the sky.

V. 274–291

At dawn Troilus summons Pandarus

I shall not see tomorrow

So let me tell you what I wish
By way of burial and inscription.
Do what you think best with my goods but of the pyre
The feast and the funeral games
Ensure that all is nobly done.
Place the powder of my burnt heart
In a gold urn and deliver it to her.

V. 295–315

Troilus makes arrangements

A diversion

We must drive these ten days ahead of us.
This city is full of pleasure pots. I know a place
Where every imaginable delicacy is served
And where all pleasing instruments
Are tuned to an ultimate sweetness.
The air has never been so provoked.
You will thrum like a plucked string.

V. 393–48

Pandarus attempts to restore Troilus

After three days

Troilus cannot stand to hear another tune.
Every woman there has been told his story.
He recites old letters as if they were prayers
And imposes her form.
He's a locked room.
They ride for home. He starts to sing.
The key is elsewhere.

V. 456–504

As if in passing

They find themselves below her window:
Barred, tight shut. He feels a frost
And rides off before anyone can see in his face
That he is as this house
Once the best of all possible places.
Then he goes to the gates by which his life left
And replays it.

V. 525–607

Himself imagined

A loss of stature, a contorted face.

Spoken of in whispers as he passes. He knows

What they say: that he's in the grip of the most

Tremendous hope and dread.

It looks to them like delusion.

He hides his subject in verse.

Long songs he sings to no one.

V. 617–637

With each day Troilus lessens

Guarded

Upon the other side remains Criseyde
With few women, among many men.
There is nothing to say to her father
That will obtain her release. If she escapes
She might be killed or raped and even if she made her way
Home – no one would be pleased.
Wouldn't he have given up already?

V. 687–706, IF *VI. 1*

With each day Criseyde doubts herself more

Out of all cure

She gazes at the distant towers of the city.
How quickly her life
Has arranged itself in scenes
Distant as memory.
How to get back inside?
She had thought it a fortress
And so it is.

V. 710–733

In conclusion

Before she is ready to act
Someone will loosen the knot.
The closed city and her estranged love
Will pass through her mind
Without catch
Like the smoothest thread
Through the eye of a needle.

V. 750–770

Criseyde decides to try to escape but

Cast

They will say that Diomede was robust
And Troilus the very measure of a man. That Criseyde
Was known to bind with golden thread
The blonde braid that hung down her back.
That she had no like, no lack
Though much will be made of her sliding courage.
No one is sure of her age.

V. 799–840

A branch about to bud

He contrives to find her alone.
She serves spice cakes and wine.
When their conversation turns to the war
He asks for her opinion
And more: are Greek ways so foreign?
And why has her father not found her a suitor?
She doesn't know what he means.

V. 841–863

Each day Diomede visits Criseyde

He bursts into blossom

Your father's dreadful vision was so clear
That when I heard he had a daughter
I myself offered to bring you here
And now I must urge you to empty your heart
Of one who has no future.
Do not waste one quarter of a single tear.
The salt will only redden your lovely face.

V. 897–917

With these words he colours a little

He turns away, pauses, rouses himself
And looks straight at her as he speaks of
The kingdom that would be his
Had his father not been killed.
He says everything that can be said:
That there is a more perfect kind of love
And that this is his first such promise.

V. 918–940

Each of his points is met

I love the place where I was born.
There are men there who are your equal.
I pray things will not fall out as you predict.
I do not doubt you'd serve a lady well.
I had a husband who died
Since when my heart has been a shell.

Who does this lie protect?

V. 955–978

Criseyde omits

So it happens

I spend the time left to me in regret
While you, a man, are free to act
So let me at least say this:
If I see what I never thought to see
I might do what I never thought to do.
I do not say I will give you my love
And I do not say I will not.

V. 988–1004

Criseyde listens again

Twilight

All day they sit and when he rises to leave
He cannot resist a little more talk.
She knows him now a man made for women.
He presses his case gently enough
And when they part she gives him a glove
Which she tells herself she does
So as not to give him her hand.

V. 1009–1015

Rarely have the stars seemed so clear

She stands beneath the rising moon
As it leaves behind the sign of the lion.
Who's counting?
From then on he speaks to her each day
And what he says draws out her pain
Bends her heart and turns her desire
From Troy (so far away now, so close to its end).

V. 1016–1036

Since there is no other way

Some say the Greek carried a pennant on his spear
Which she had sewn from her sleeve.
That he captured Troilus's bay and gave it to her.
That she gave it back but washed his wounds.
That she gave up.
No one's sure how long it took her to succumb.
If you've heard her name you know what she's done.

V. 1037–1069

On the tenth day

They climb the city walls to look for her coming.
All manner of person who appears on the horizon
Has to be her. Until they are not. He studies
Each tree and grove and hedge, craning his neck.

There she is at last!

All his friend sees is a cart
Being hauled from place to place.

V. 1105–62

Troilus and Pandarus go to meet Criseyde

Turning for home

He decides she must be waiting for dark
And then when every star is out
That he has made a mistake.
What she really meant was that she'd be back
When the moon has passed beyond
The sign of the ram – which is when?
Next day up and down the walls again.

V. 1165–1194

Troilus reconfigures

He has lost the thing that gave his life its frame

Three, four, five, six days pass
And each day he recovers her promise
Only to feel it break again
And desire rise through his pain
And with it his tears.
He flees from company, from comfort, from life
As from fire.

V. 1199–1218

His manliness

The shame is crippling.
He uses a stick to stagger about
Exhausted.
The king, his mother, brothers and sisters
Beg to know what's wrong.
He says he has a disease of the heart.
A defect that will kill him.

V. 1219–1232

A clearing

He dreams a dense forest
A crash and roar
And the charge of a great boar
And Criseyde caught beneath its feet
And how it cut out her heart with its teeth
And taking her in its arms lay down to sleep
And how this pleased her.

V. 1233–1241, IF *VII. 23, 24*

Out of sleep

Now I see clearly
She will not come. What has she left
To offer? What subtle pleasure
What contempt, what perversity
Has turned her from me?
What did she mean?
Nothing?

V. 1243–1260

Troilus remembers his dream

A clause

What you believe you need to know
So write. Ask if she has reason not to come.
If she doesn't reply you will have your answer.
If she does then we can read true cause
Between her lines.

The prince sits down to turn over the matter
Of how best to describe his suffering.

V. 1291–1316

Pandarus suggests that Troilus sends a letter

Pages

My bewildered soul commends itself . . .
Some time past you left . . . and have not
. . . This agony compels me . . .
Two months now . . . day by day I want more not less . . .
. . . To know why and if you have chosen this . . .
. . . Still my breath . . .
Tell me. End this.

V. 1317–1407

She cannot say when

She will come

As soon as she can and all will be mended.

He shakes out her words:

Flattery, promises, nothing.

The truce is over.

Troilus starts up like a famished lion

Who has glimpsed a boar.

V. 1424–1431, IF *VII. 80*

Eventually Criseyde sends a note

Permutation

All things are committed to exchange
And so his grief becomes a kind of strength
Just as the ground starts to give way.
The gods have ordained
That Troy's every bright feather be plucked
And that this once great city
Will go unnamed.

V. 1534–1547

The death of Hector

The hero catches up with his life's end
On a muddy field. Preoccupied
With a man he is dragging by the throat
He does not see the tireless Achilles.
Troilus, who has learnt to accommodate grief,
Makes more room for it.
An added depth.

V. 1548–1568

His heart begins to repair

With hope almost gone he is restored to love.
It is who he is.
He finds new excuses
And thinks to disguise himself
And slip into the enemy camp as a pilgrim.
But who would not recognise him?
He writes to her often and at length.

V. 1571–1583

207]

Her last words

I cannot heal your pain. I have my own.
You send me all these pages yet offer me nothing.
There are matters I dare not mention
Which hold me in this place.
I will come but cannot give a date.
Judge me by my intent and not this letter's length.
Speak well of me. Be my friend.

V. 1590–1630

Disjunct

He cannot make sense of her letter.
It sits before him like the first page
Of a calendar for a year so new
That nothing has yet been named.
She addresses him as if he were a stranger
With the kindness of politeness.
He no longer believes her.

V. 1632–1645

A clasp

What brings it home
Is Deiphebe parading through the town
The tunic he has torn from a Greek that day
Which Troilus takes up so as to praise the spoils.
Remarking on its length and breadth and detail
He runs the cloth between his fingers
Which catch on what held the tunic in place.

V. 1650–1661

Heartless

Was this not the ruby heart
She had given him? Had he not
Given it back at their parting?
She had taken it as she might a vow
And she had given it to the man
From whom it had been taken now
To be handed among the crowd.

V. 1661–1694

An ending

This is how she delivers her message.
I have been displaced.
Cast clean out of her mind.
I will kill him or he will kill me.
Either way may the gods take notice
And force her to take notice.
I still do not know how to unlove her.

V. 1681–1708

All this he says to Pandarus

An audience

His friend is without reply.
He cannot feign surprise
So curses his niece and wishes her dead
But knows it meaningless.
It's as if his part in all this
Has been only to say the right words.
He has no more words.

V. 1723–1743

He seeks the story of his death

He scours the field in search of Diomede.
They clash often
Throw taunts, lob heavy blows
Test the sharpness of their spears.
Each draws the other's blood
But this is out of their hands.
They survive one another.

V. 1755–1764

That he is slain in this manner

The battle staggers on through this day.
No one advances and nothing is gained.
Running with blood
The enemies are at deadlock
When Achilles comes across the crazed prince
And slits his throat
Almost as an afterthought.

V. 1800–1806

What he notices

How lightly his spirit escapes his body
And lifts into infinite space.
How clearly he can now see
The scale and alignment of all things
And that this is the music
That has lain for so long
Beyond him.

V. 1808–1813

He is his own happiness

He looks down on what he has left:
A spot of earth
Embraced by the sea
A city
A camp close by
A field where men weep
And he laughs.

V. 1814–1821